MEDIUM VOICE

Voices of Praise

VOCAL • PIANO

T0052917

ISBN 0-634-08939-0

HAL•LEONARD®
CORPORATION

7777 W. BLUEMOUND RD. P.O. BOX 13819
MILWAUKEE, WISCONSIN 53213

For all works contained herein:
Unauthorized copying, arranging, adapting, recording
or public performance is an infringement of copyright.
Infringers are liable under the law.

Visit Hal Leonard Online at
www.halleonard.com

PAGE	SONG TITLE	VOCAL DEMO TRACK*	ACCOMPANIMENT TRACK
4	GOD WILL MAKE A WAY	1	11
10	HE KNOWS MY NAME	2	12
13	HERE I AM TO WORSHIP	3	13
18	I WORSHIP YOU, ALMIGHTY GOD	4	14
26	LORD MOST HIGH	5	15
30	OPEN THE EYES OF MY HEART	6	16
36	RISE UP AND PRAISE HIM	7	17
42	THERE IS NONE LIKE YOU	8	18
52	WE ALL BOW DOWN	9	19
45	WORTHY IS THE LAMB	10	20

* The vocal demo tracks have been shortened due to space limitations on the CD.

God Will Make A Way

as recorded by Don Moen

Words and Music by
Don Moen

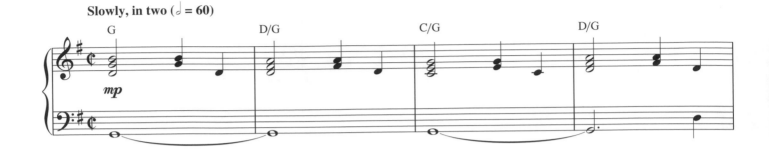

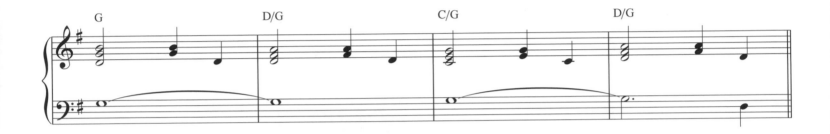

God will make __ a way __ where there seems to be __ no way. __ He

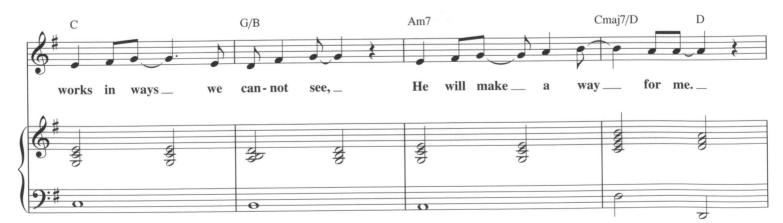

works in ways __ we can-not see, __ He will make __ a way __ for me. __

© 1990 Integrity's Hosanna! Music/ASCAP
c/o Integrity Media, Inc., 1000 Cody Road, Mobile, AL 36695
All Rights Reserved   International Copyright Secured   Used by Permission

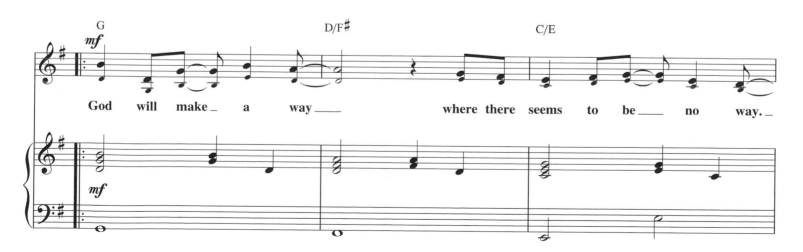

road - way in __ the wil - der - ness __ He'll lead __ me, and

riv - ers in __ the des - ert will _ I see. __

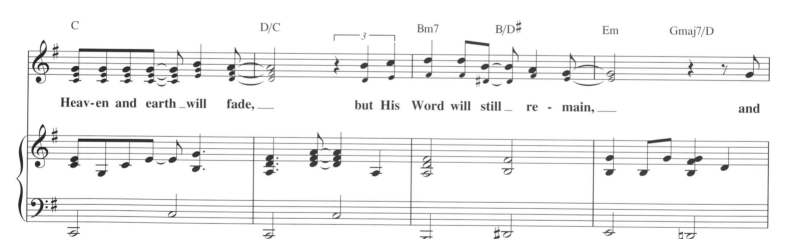

Heav-en and earth _ will fade, __ but His Word will still _ re - main, __ and

He will do __ some - thing new __ to - day. __ Oh,

Oh, God will make a way

where there seems to be no way. He

works in ways we can - not see, He will make a way for me.

He will be my guide, hold me close - ly to His side, with

love and strength _ for each new day, _ He will make _ a way, _

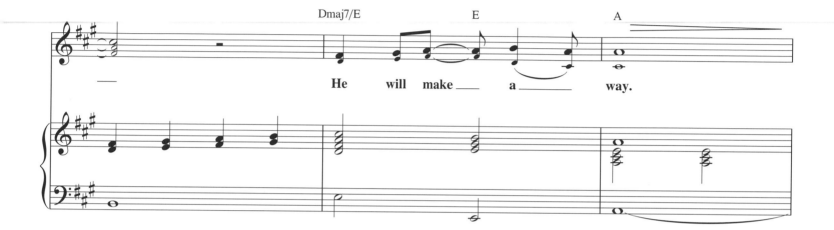

_ He will make _ a _ way.

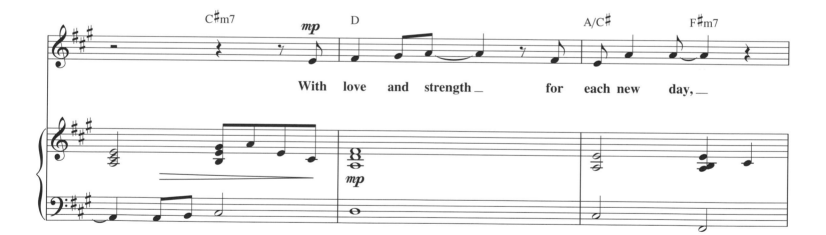

With love and strength _ for each new day, _

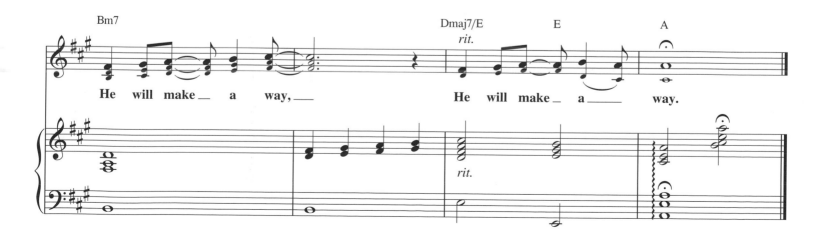

He will make _ a way, _ He will make _ a _ way.

He Knows My Name

as recorded by Tommy Walker

Words and Music by
Tommy Walker

© 1996 DOULOS PUBLISHING (Administered by THE COPYRIGHT COMPANY, Nashville, TN)
All Rights Reserved   International Copyright Secured   Used by Permission

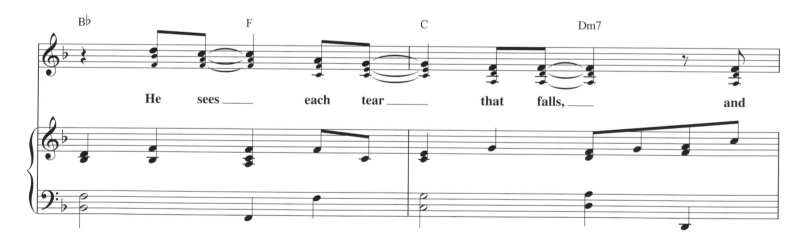

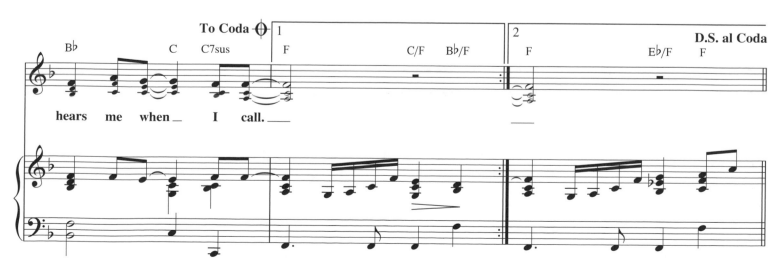

CODA

Slower, rubato

And He knows _ your name, _____

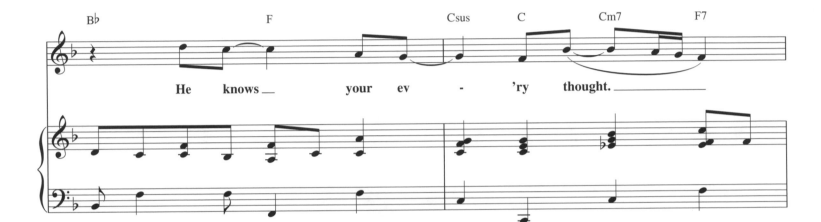

He knows _ your ev - 'ry thought. _____

He sees _ all those tears _____ that _ fall, and He'll

molto rit.

hear you when you call. ___

Here I Am To Worship

as recorded by the Integrity Worship Singers

Words and Music by
Tim Hughes

Light of the world, You stepped down in - to dark - ness,
o - pened my eyes, let me
King of all days, oh, so high - ly ex - alt - ed,
glo - rious in heav - en a -

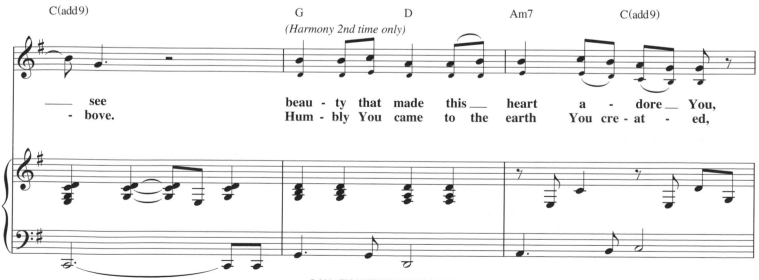

—— see
- bove.

beau - ty that made this —— heart a - dore —— You,
Hum - bly You came to the earth You cre - at - ed,

© 2001 THANKYOU MUSIC (PRS)
Admin. Worldwide excluding the UK and Europe by WORSHIPTOGETHER.COM SONGS (ASCAP)
Admin. in the UK and Europe by KINGSWAY MUSIC
All Rights Reserved   Used by Permission

hope of a life spent with ____ You. ____
all for love's sake be - came ___ poor. ____

Here I am to

wor - ship, here I am to bow down, here I am to say that You're my God. __

__ You're al - to - geth - er love - ly, al - to - geth - er wor - thy, al - to - geth - er

won - der - ful to me. __

And I'll nev -

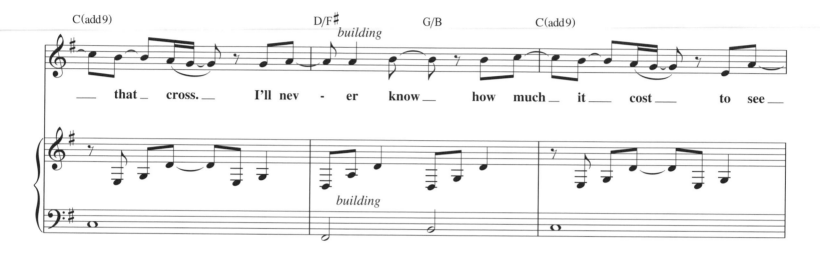

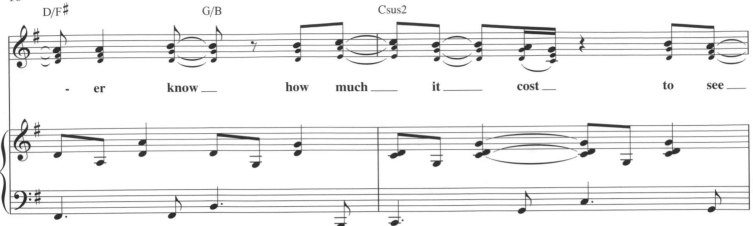

-er know __ how much __ it __ cost __ to see __

__ my sin __ up-on __ that __ cross. __ Here I am to

Here I am to wor-ship, here I am to

bow down, here I am to say that You're my God. __ You're al-to-geth-er

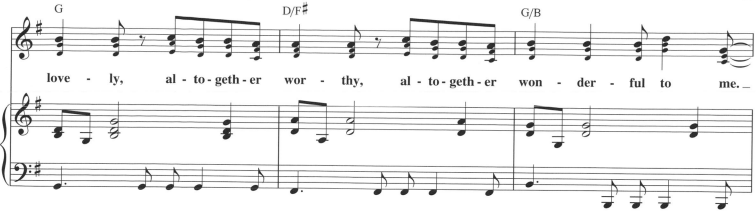

love - ly, al - to - geth - er wor - thy, al - to - geth - er won - der - ful to me. _

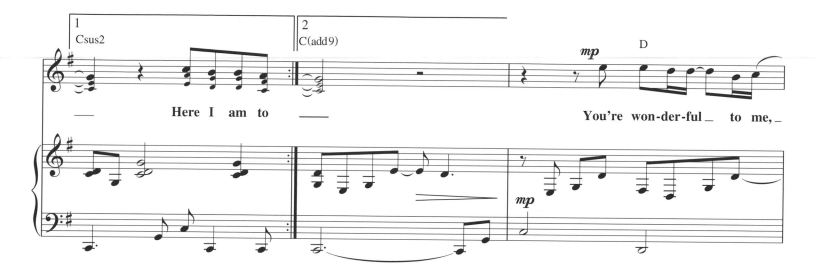

1 Csus2 — Here I am to —

2 C(add9) You're won-der-ful _ to me, _

D *mp*

C(add9) _____

D *freely* Light _ of the world, _____

C(add9) King of _ all days, _

D You _ are glo - ri - ous. _____

C(add9)

D

Csus2(#4)

I Worship You, Almighty God

as recorded by the Integrity Worship Singers

Words and Music by
Sondra Corbett-Wood

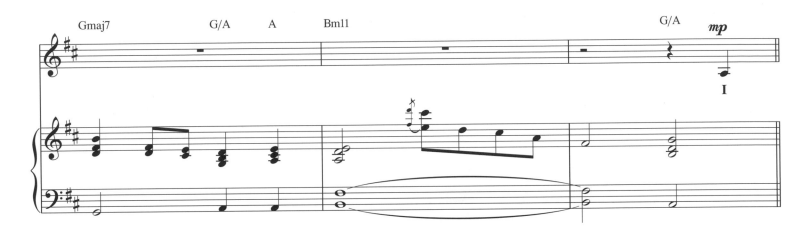

wor - ship You, Al - might - y God, there is none like

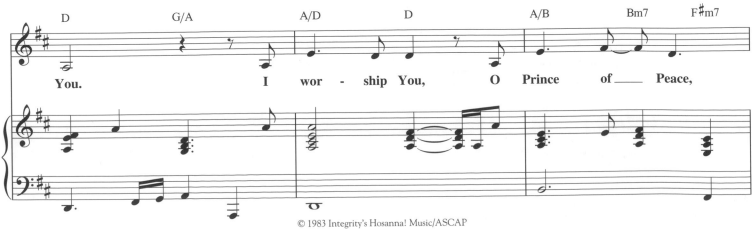

You. I wor - ship You, O Prince of ____ Peace,

© 1983 Integrity's Hosanna! Music/ASCAP
c/o Integrity Media, Inc., 1000 Cody Road, Mobile, AL 36695
All Rights Reserved   International Copyright Secured   Used by Permission

that is what I want to ____ do. I give You ___ praise, _____

____ for You are my right - eous - ness. _____ I

wor - ship You, Al - might - y ___ God, __ there is none like ___

You. I wor - ship You, Al - might - y God,

there is none like You. I wor - ship You, O

Prince of ___ Peace, that is what I want to do. I

give You praise, _____ for You are my right - eous - ness.

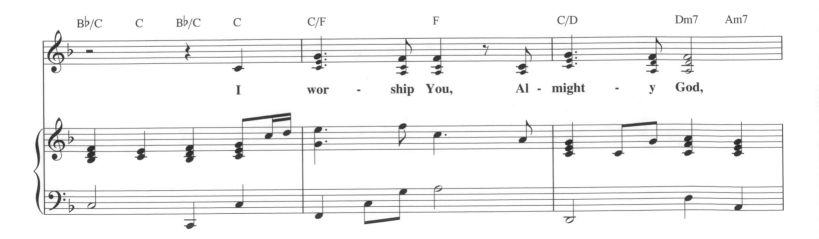

I wor - ship You, Al - might - y God,

there is none like You, there is none like You.

Ladies
There is none like

Men
There is none, there is none like

You.

You.

I wor - ship You, Al -

might - y God, there is none like You._____ I

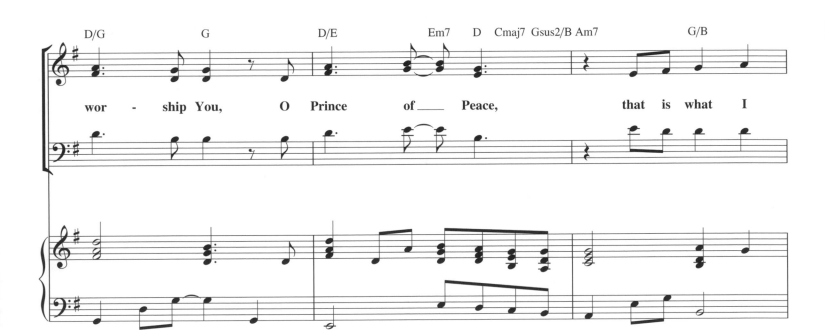

wor - ship You, O Prince of ___ Peace, that is what I

want to do. I give You praise, _____ for You are my

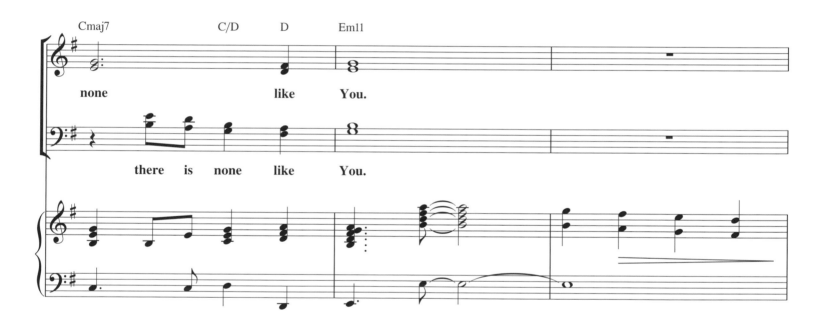

Lord Most High

as recorded by Ross Parsley

Words and Music by Don Harris
and Gary Sadler

© 1996 Integrity's Hosanna! Music/ASCAP
c/o Integrity Media, Inc., 1000 Cody Road, Mobile, AL 36695
All Rights Reserved   International Copyright Secured   Used by Permission

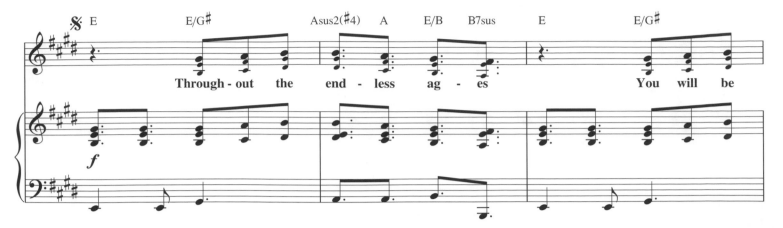

Through - out the end - less ag - es   You will be

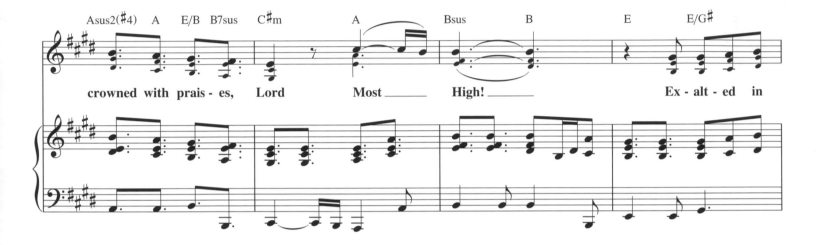

crowned with prais - es, Lord   Most_____ High!_____   Ex - alt - ed in

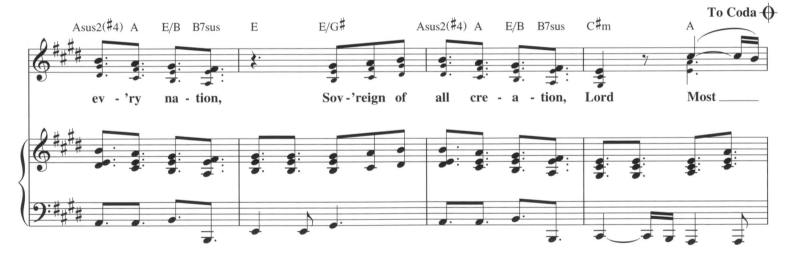

ev - 'ry na - tion,   Sov - 'reign of all cre - a - tion, Lord   Most_____

High,   be mag - ni -fied! __   From the   High!_____

CODA

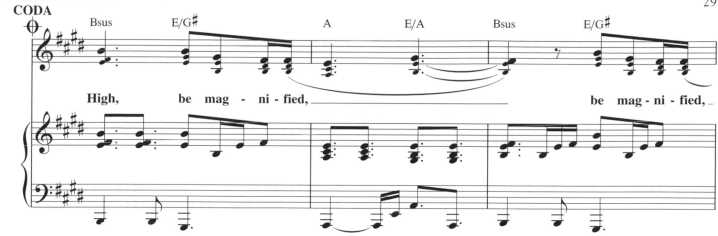

High, be mag - ni - fied, _____ be mag - ni - fied, _

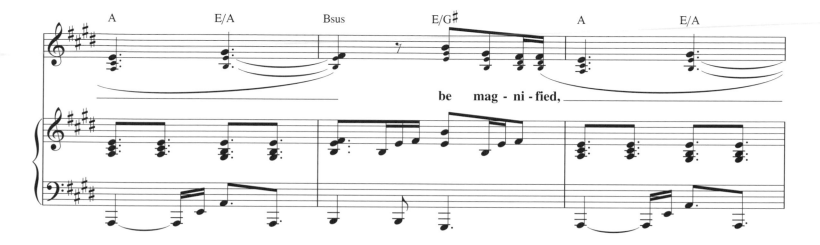

be mag - ni - fied, _____

be mag - ni - fied, _____ be mag - ni - fied, _

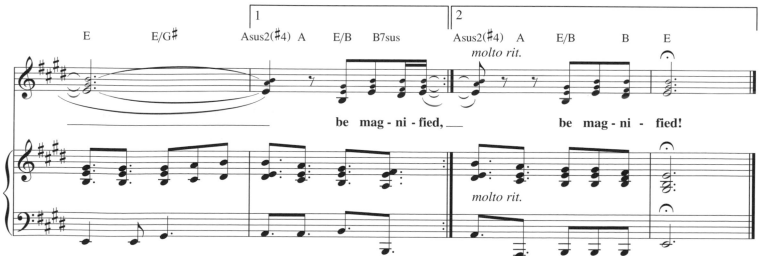

be mag - ni - fied, ___ be mag - ni - fied!

Open The Eyes Of My Heart

as recorded by Paul Baloche

Words and Music by
Paul Baloche

© 1997 Integrity's Hosanna! Music/ASCAP
c/o Integrity Media, Inc., 1000 Cody Road, Mobile, AL 36695
All Rights Reserved   International Copyright Secured   Used by Permission

O - pen the eyes _ of my heart, ___ Lord. _   O - pen the eyes _ of my heart. _

_   I want _ to see You, _   I want _ to

see You. _   To see You

high and lift - ed up, ___ shin - ing in the light of Your glo -

Pour out __ Your pow'r and love, __ as we sing

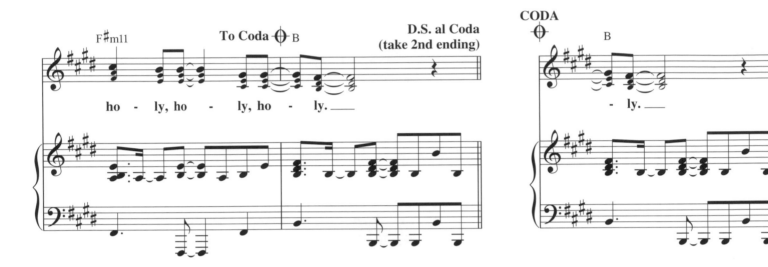

ho - ly, ho - ly, ho - ly. __

- ly. __

High and lift - ed up, __ shin - ing in the light of Your glo -

- ry. __ Pour out __ Your pow'r and love, __ as we sing

ho - ly, ho - ly, ho - ly. ____

Ho - ly, ho - ly, ho - ly, ____ ho - ly, ho - ly, ho -

- ly, ____ ho - ly, ho - ly, ho - ly; ____ I want __ to

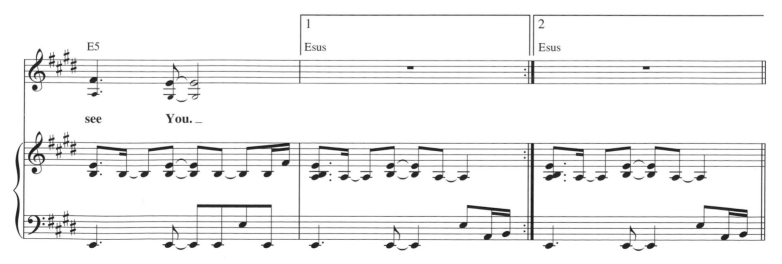

see You. __

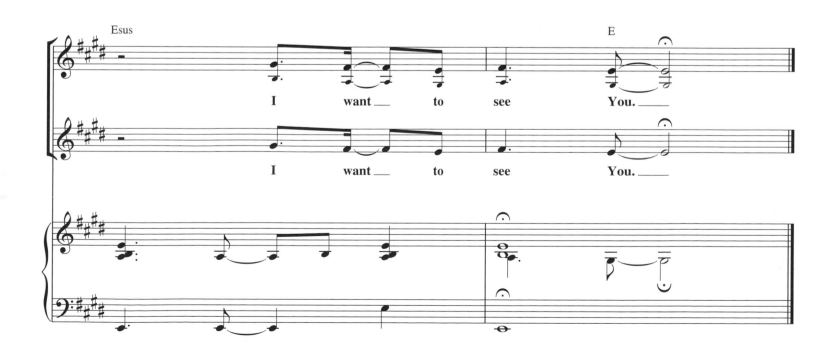

Rise Up And Praise Him

as recorded by Paul Baloche

Words and Music by Paul Baloche
and Gary Sadler

Driving (♩ = 144)

Let the heav-ens re-joice, let the earth be glad. Let the peo-ple of God sing His praise all o-ver the land.

© 1996 Integrity's Hosanna! Music/ASCAP
c/o Integrity Media, Inc., 1000 Cody Road, Mobile, AL 36695
All Rights Reserved   International Copyright Secured   Used by Permission

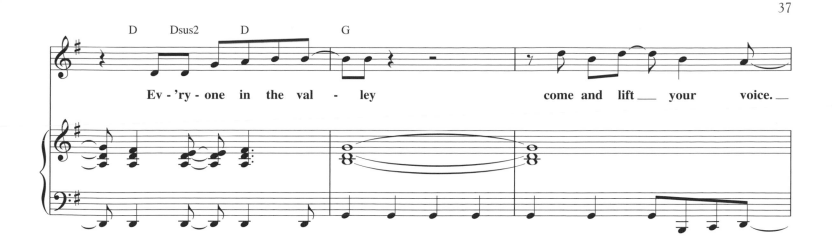

Ev-'ry-one in the val - ley come and lift___ your voice.___

___ All those___ on the moun - tain - top___ be ___ glad

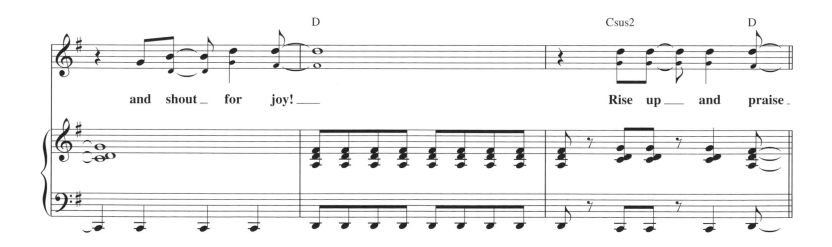

and shout___ for joy! ___ Rise up___ and praise___

___ Him, He de - serves___ our ___ love. ___

Rise up __ and praise __ Him, wor-ship the Ho-

- ly _____ One with all __ your heart, with all __ your soul,

with all __ your might. __ Rise up __ and praise _

__ Him! _

Let the heav-ens re - joice, ___ Rise up ___ and praise ___

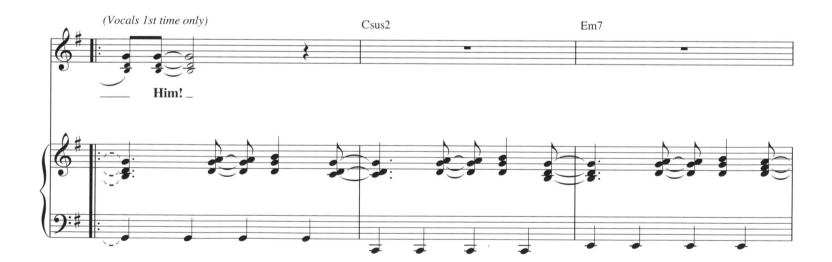

(Vocals 1st time only)

___ Him! _

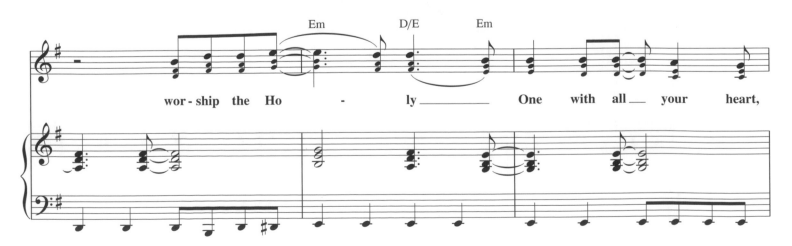

with all __ your soul, with all __ your might. __

Rise up __ and praise __ Him!

Rise up __ and praise __ Rise up __ and praise __

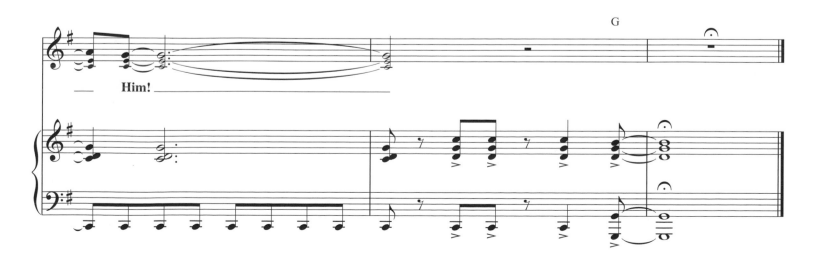

__ Him! _____

There Is None Like You

as recorded by Lenny LeBlanc

Words and Music by
Lenny LeBlanc

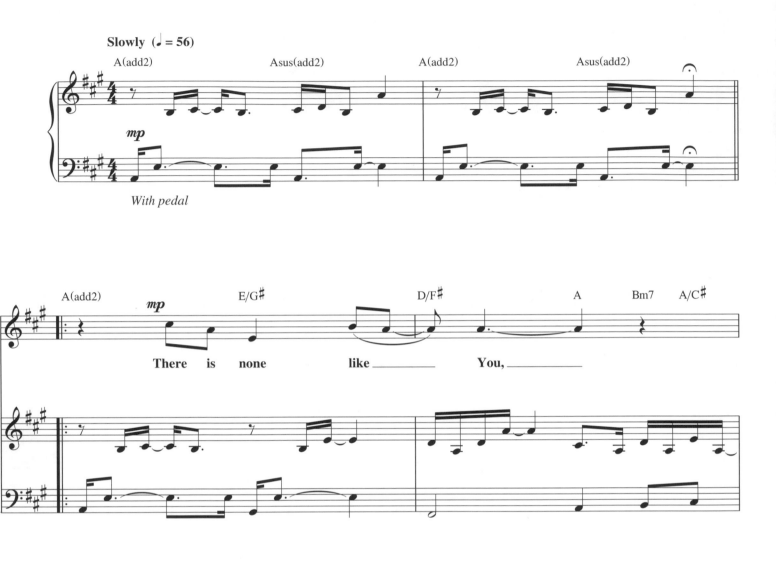

Lyrics: There is none like You, no one else can touch my heart like You do.

© 1991 Integrity's Hosanna! Music/ASCAP
c/o Integrity Media, Inc., 1000 Cody Road, Mobile, AL 36695
All Rights Reserved   International Copyright Secured   Used by Permission

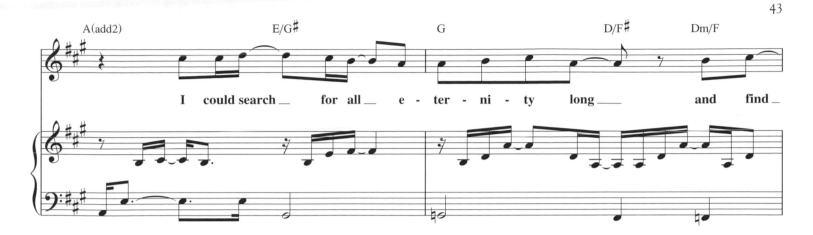

I could search __ for all __ e - ter - ni - ty long ____ and find __

__ there is none like _____ You.

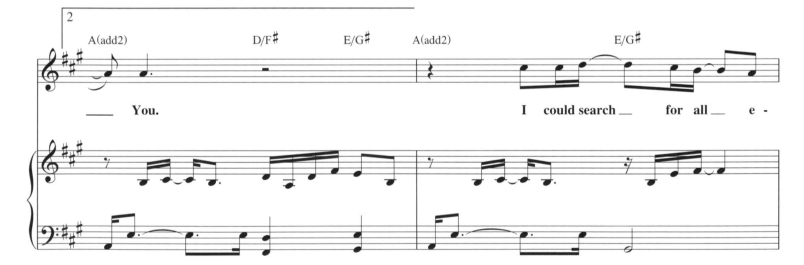

__ You.   I could search __ for all __ e -

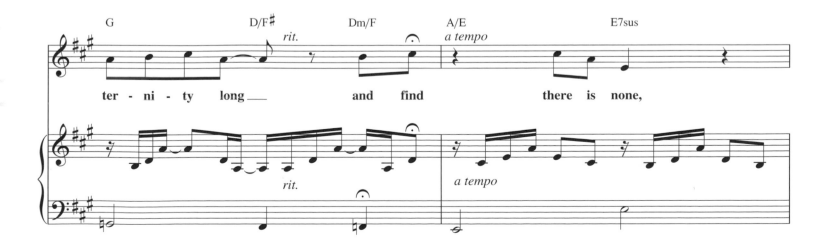

ter - ni - ty long ____ and find   there is none,

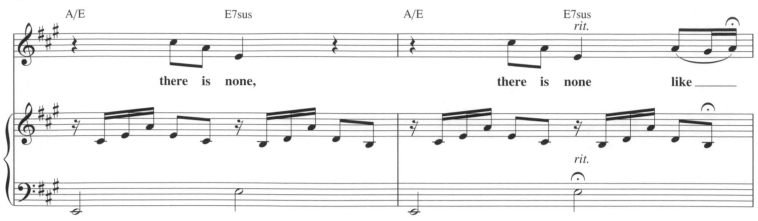

there is none, there is none like _____

You. _____

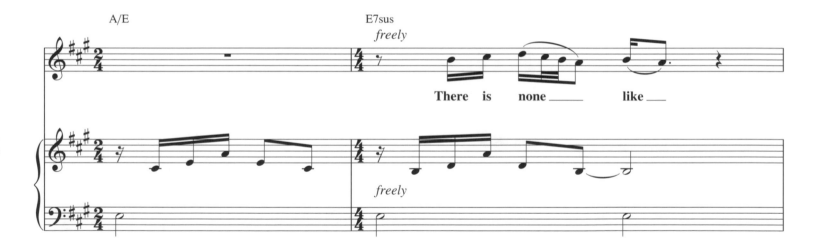

There is none _____ like _____

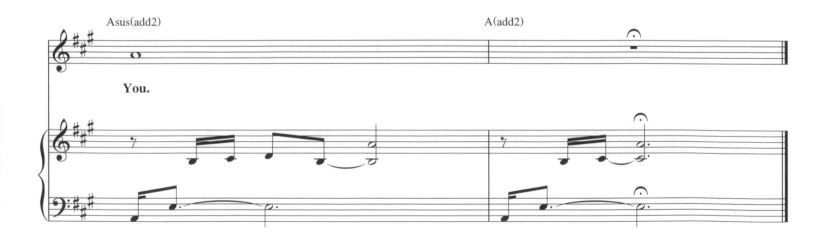

You.

Worthy Is The Lamb
(With "Crown Him With Many Crowns")
as recorded by Travis Cottrell

Words and Music by
Darlene Zschech

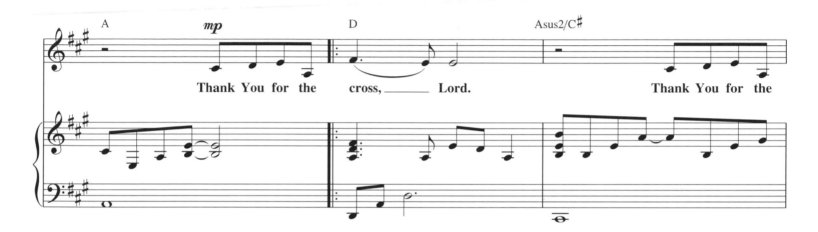

Thank You for the cross, _____ Lord. Thank You for the

price You paid. ___ Bear-ing all my sin and _ shame, _ in

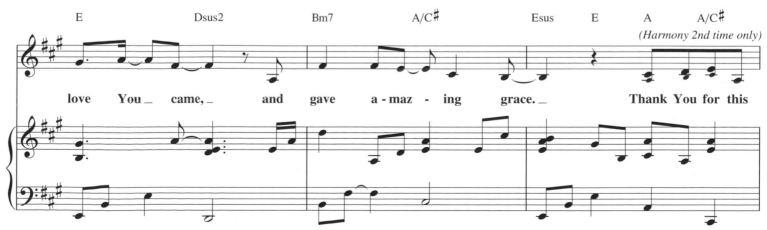

love You _ came, _ and gave a - maz - ing grace. _ Thank You for this

© 2000 Darlene Zschech and Hillsong Publishing (admin. in the U.S. and Canada by Integrity's Hosanna! Music/ASCAP)
c/o Integrity Media, Inc., 1000 Cody Road, Mobile, AL 36695
All Rights Reserved International Copyright Secured Used by Permission

Crown You now _ with man - y crowns, _ You reign vic - to - ri - ous. _

_ High and lift - ed up, _

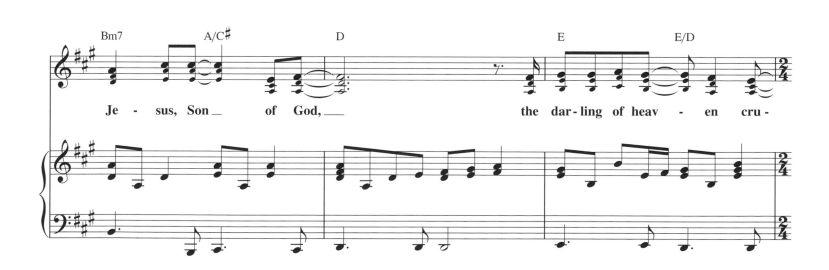

Je - sus, Son _ of God, _ the dar - ling of heav - en cru -

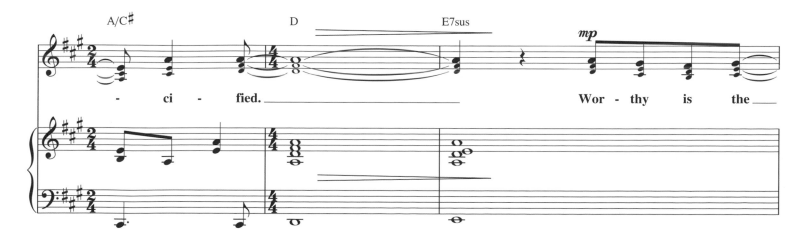

- ci - fied. _ Wor - thy is the _

CROWN HIM WITH MANY CROWNS
Words by MATTHEW BRIDGES
Music by GEORGE JOB ELVEY

Arr. © 2003 Integrity's Hosanna! Music/ASCAP
c/o Integrity Media, Inc., 1000 Cody Road, Mobile, AL 36695
All Rights Reserved   International Copyright Secured   Used by Permission

match - less King through all e - ter - ni - ty.

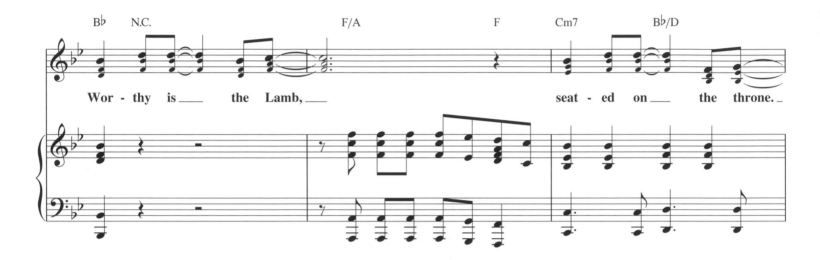

Wor - thy is___ the Lamb,___ seat - ed on___ the throne.___

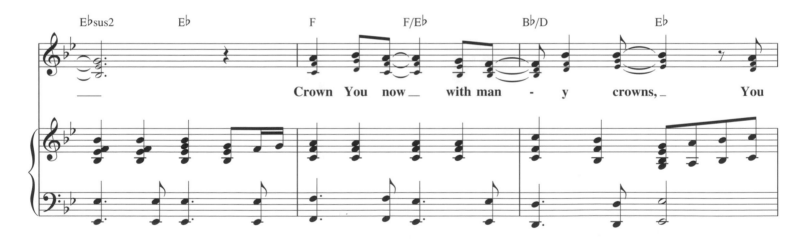

___ Crown You now___ with man - y crowns,___ You

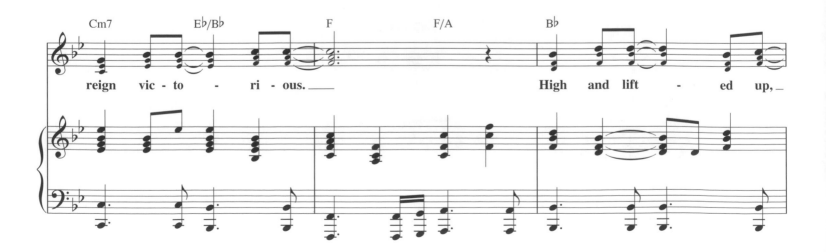

reign vic - to - ri - ous.___ High and lift - ed up,___

51

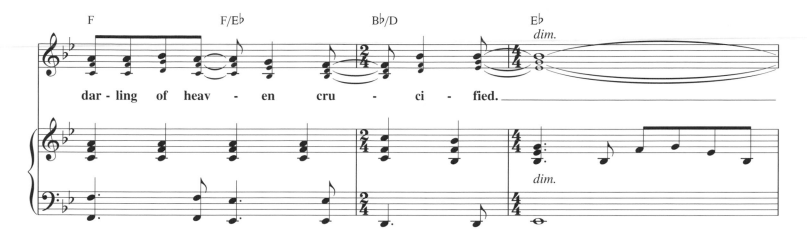

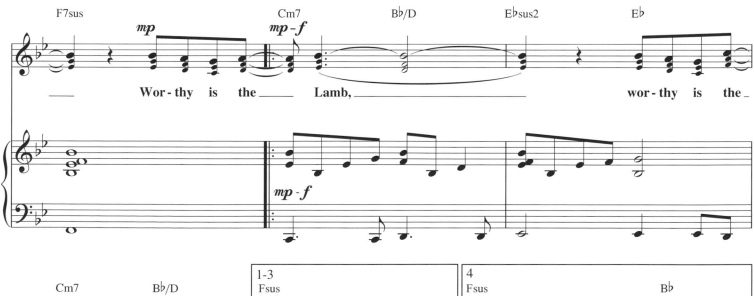

We All Bow Down

as recorded by the Integrity Worship Singers

Words and Music by
Lenny LeBlanc

© 2002 Integrity's Hosanna! Music/ASCAP (c/o Integrity Media, Inc., 1000 Cody Road, Mobile, AL 36695) and LenSongs Publishing/ASCAP
All Rights Reserved   International Copyright Secured   Used by Permission

all bow down. _ Kings will sur - ren - der their crowns _

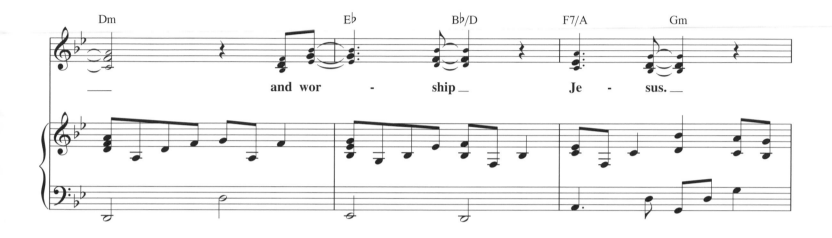

_ and wor - ship _ Je - sus. _

He is the love, _ un - fail - ing love, _____ He is the love _ of

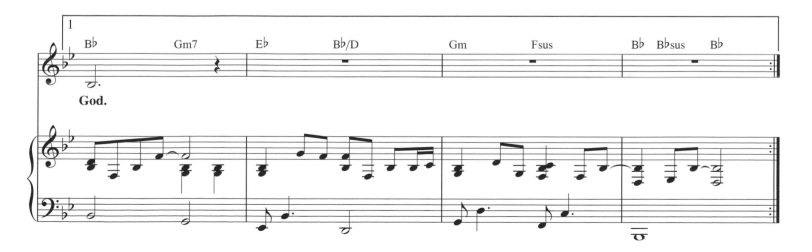

God.

God. He is the light of ___ the world _____ and

Lord of ___ the cross. _____

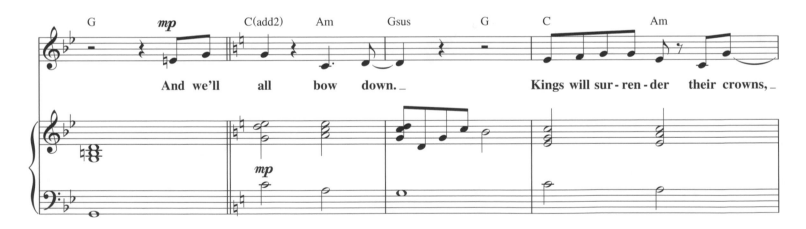

And we'll all bow down. _ Kings will sur-ren-der their crowns, _

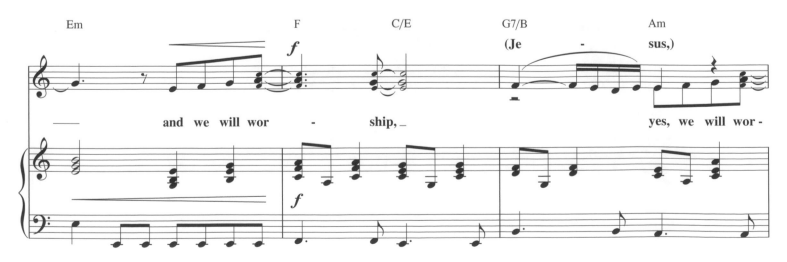

___ and we will wor - ship, _ (Je - sus,) yes, we will wor-

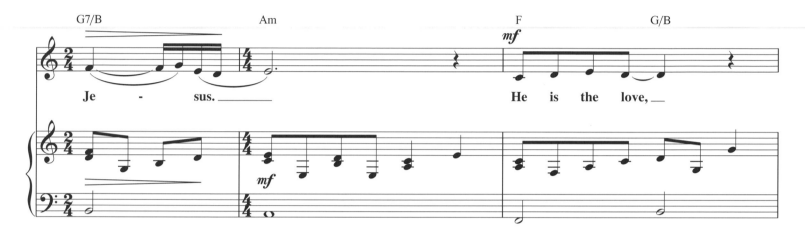

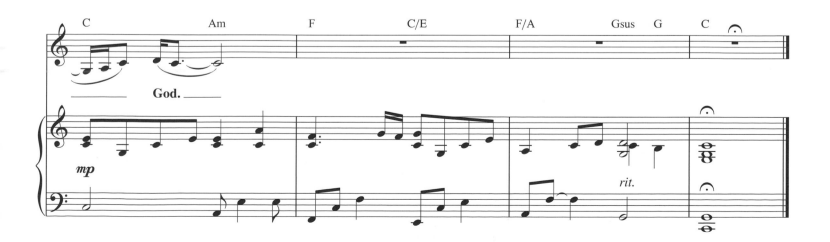

THE BEST PRAISE & WORSHIP SONGBOOKS

THE BEST OF PAUL BALOCHE – OPEN THE EYES OF MY HEART

This songbook features 12 of Paul's best praise & worship favorites: Above All • All the Earth Will Sing Your Praises • Arise • Celebrate the Lord of Love • I Love to Be in Your Presence • I See the Lord • Offering • Open the Eyes of My Heart • Praise Adonai • Revival Fire Fall • Rise Up and Praise Him • Sing Out.
08739746 Piano/Vocal/Guitar $14.95

THE BEST OF HILLSONG

25 of the most popular songs from Hillsong artists and writers, including: All Things Are Possible • Awesome in This Place • Blessed • Eagle's Wings • God Is Great • Holy Spirit Rain Down • I Give You My Heart • Jesus, What a Beautiful Name • The Potter's Hand • Shout to the Lord • Worthy Is the Lamb • You Are Near • and more.
08739789 Piano/Vocal/Guitar $16.95

THE BEST OF INTEGRITY MUSIC

25 of the best praise & worship songs from Integrity: Ancient of Days • Celebrate Jesus • Firm Foundation • Give Thanks • Mighty Is Our God • Open the Eyes of My Heart • Trading My Sorrows • You Are Good • and more.
08739790 Piano/Vocal/Guitar $16.95

THE BEST OF MODERN WORSHIP

15 of today's most powerful worship songs: Cannot Say Enough • Everyday • Fields of Grace • Freedom • Friend of God • God Is Great • Here I Am to Worship • I Can Only Imagine • Lord, You Have My Heart • Meet with Me • Open the Eyes of My Heart • Sing for Joy • Trading My Sorrows • Word of God Speak • You Are My King (Amazing Love).
08739747 Piano/Vocal/Guitar $14.95

COME INTO HIS PRESENCE

Features 12 beautiful piano solo arrangements of worship favorites: Above All • Blessed Be the Lord God Almighty • Breathe • Come Into His Presence • Draw Me Close • Give Thanks • God Will Make a Way • Jesus, Name Above All Names/Blessed Be the Name of the Lord • Lord Have Mercy • More Precious Than Silver • Open the Eyes of My Heart • Shout to the Lord.
08739299 Piano Solo..$12.95

GIVE THANKS – THE BEST OF HOSANNA! MUSIC

This superb best-of collection features 25 worship favorites published by Hosanna! Music: Ancient of Days • Celebrate Jesus • I Worship You, Almighty God • More Precious Than Silver • My Redeemer Lives • Shout to the Lord • and more.
08739729 Piano/Vocal/Guitar $14.95
08739745 Easy Piano..$12.95

iWORSHIP CHRISTMAS

Selections from the popular Christmas album, including: Away in a Manger • The Birthday of a King • Breath of Heaven (Mary's Song) • Come, Thou Long-Expected Jesus • Hallelujah • Joy to the World/Heaven and Nature Sing • One Small Child/More Precious Than Silver • What Child Is This? • You Are Emmanuel/Emmanuel • and more.
08739788 Piano/Vocal/Guitar $16.95

THE SONGS OF MERCYME – I CAN ONLY IMAGINE

10 of the most recognizable songs from this popular Contemporary Christian group, including the smash hit "I Can Only Imagine," plus: Cannot Say Enough • Here with Me • Homesick • How Great Is Your Love • The Love of God • Spoken For • Unaware • Where You Lead Me • Word of God Speak.
08739803 Piano Solo..$12.95

MERCYME – 20 FAVORITES

A jam-packed collection of 20 of their best. Includes: Crazy • Go • Here with Me • I Can Only Imagine • In the Blink of an Eye • Never Alone • On My Way to You • Spoken For • Undone • Word of God Speak • Your Glory Goes On • and more.
08739862 Piano/Vocal/Guitar $16.95

Prices, contents & availability subject to change without notice.

FOR MORE INFORMATION, SEE YOUR LOCAL MUSIC DEALER, OR WRITE TO:

HAL•LEONARD® CORPORATION
7777 W. BLUEMOUND RD. P.O. BOX 13819 MILWAUKEE, WI 53213

Complete songlists available online at
www.halleonard.com

MIGHTY IS OUR GOD

25 beloved praise & worship songs, including: Above All • Firm Foundation • I Stand in Awe • Lord Most High • Open the Eyes of My Heart • Sing for Joy • Think About His Love • and more.
08739744 Piano/Vocal/Guitar $14.95

THE BEST OF DON MOEN – GOD WILL MAKE A WAY

19 of the greatest hits from this Dove Award-winning singer/songwriter. Includes: Celebrate Jesus • God Will Make a Way • Here We Are • I Will Sing • Let Your Glory Fall • Shout to the Lord • We Give You Glory • You Make Me Lie Down in Green Pastures • and more.
08739297 Piano/Vocal/Guitar $16.95

PHILLIPS, CRAIG & DEAN – LET THE WORSHIPPERS ARISE

12 songs from the 2004 release by this trio of pastors. Includes: Because I'm Forgiven • You Are God Alone • Let the Worshippers Arise • My Redeemer Lives • Awake My Soul • Mighty Is the Power of the Cross • and more.
08739804 Piano/Vocal/Guitar $16.95

PIANO PRAISE

This flexible book features 8 songs for performing in church as a soloist or at home for personal worship. Includes optional instrumental obbligato parts, chord symbols for improvisation, and a CD with play-along tracks and demonstrations. Includes: Firm Foundation • Jesus, Name Above All Names • More Precious Than Silver • Open the Eyes of My Heart • and more.
08739851 Piano Solo – Book/CD Pack................$19.95

VOICES OF PRAISE

10 worship favorites arranged especially for vocalists, including: God Will Make a Way • Here I Am to Worship • Open the Eyes of My Heart • and more. The CD includes vocal demonstrations as well as accompaniment tracks.
08739801 Medium Voice – Book/CD Pack..........$19.95

DARLENE ZSCHECH – WORTHY IS THE LAMB

15 songs from this contemporary worship leader, including: Blessed • Hallelujah • Irresistible • Kiss of Heaven • Let the Peace of God Reign • The Potter's Hand • Shout to the Lord • Worthy Is the Lamb • and more.
08739852 Piano/Vocal/Guitar $16.95